OLD PHOTOGRAPHS AND WILD DREAMS

JOHN BUCHER SR.

SIDESHOW
MEDIA GROUP

8033 SUNSET BLVD. #164   LOS ANGELES, CA. 90046

SSMG PRESS / LOS ANGELES

Old Photographs and Wild Dreams
John Bucher Sr.

SSMG Press
Sideshow Media Group
8033 Sunset Blvd. #164
Los Angeles, CA. 90046
USA
sideshowmediagroup.com

Copyright © 2019
ISBN 978-0-9971297-8-6

DEDICATED TO PATRICK MULCAHY WHO KNOWS WHY OR SHOULD

In the late nineteen nineties, during a construction boom, several blocks of a downtown Los Angeles city businesses closed their doors to make way for high rise luxury apartments, organic grocery concerns, workout spaces, and coffee shops. One of the stores scheduled for demolition was an antique shop with an eclectic array of sundries for sale. Since it was the last of a third-generation family, when faced with extinction, they were happy to retire in a sunny climate with a generous nest egg. They held a "going out of business sale" event in which every item must go.

Some large items were from old circus venues and sideshows such as authentic costumes, old swords, and historical documents. Stuffed animals sat beside some prize period furniture. After the sale was over, the shop was bare except for a stack of old dusty boxes in the storage area. The boxes were moved to the alley near the dumpsters and forgotten. That same night a windstorm attacked the city and blew the boxes into the air and all over the streets. One such box contained old photographs, some over one hundred years old. As they blew across the city and were picked up and wondered at, stories came alive and fired a few new, wild dreams. Here are those stories.

OLD
PHOTOGRAPHS
AND
WILD DREAMS

Old Photographs and Wild Dreams

The first time was special, remembering the cold
funeral in Dallas for someone not so old
Fresh from the round house, engines did race
Denison station a big scary place
Mounting wrought iron steps to find the right seat
train car so full strange rendezvous meet
Shiny steel sculpted with curtains and wood
ladies in hosiery swishing a lilac good
Hearts beat as one when the whistle blew loud
feeling the movement riding a steel cloud
Sherman came fast fields of black dirt
gentlemen in their newspapers starchy white shirts
Gathering speed across empty winter grounds
foxes dance in the sunlight scatter at the sound
So elegant a world on heavy round wheels
windows in the dining car table cloth meals
McKinney came next and then Dallas station
husbands and wives foreign relations
Riding the Katy a distant recall
dead rusty cars behind a rotting wall
A sweet part of Texas gone for the time
only in dreams can you ride the Katy line

Old Photographs and Wild Dreams

daybreak rushes in a thunder cloud mystery of
splintering rail lines
How did I get here?
Multiple hobos, dirty and scarred
…gather in handfuls
stare at my skull
memory...memory...yes...no
Walking down the cluster of rail lines
spiraling into oblivion
creosote farms of odor as hot steel
...vibrates
here comes another – climb aboard
deep in thought "I'm nothing but a road apple"
Cool wind pulls my shirt like a
kite from tomorrow
green blurs
of leafy forests invade my vision
rumble of the tracks push me into a dream state against my will
later on
hunger takes over
town up ahead...lots of lights in the darkness
my fate...destiny
maybe a bar with a lonesome soul who desires conversation
with a road apple
sad sentences revive rules
for flat lands letting
time trip by bigger
dull days
for a retiring road apple

Old Photographs and Wild Dreams

When Honest Abe was slain, the fractured
nation mourned
Prayed their broken hearts wouldn't remain so
lost and forlorn
They loaded his body on a train car dark
and somber to go home
His last train carried him to rest with the angels
who watched over his stately bones
Dressed in black with curtains made from
the country's sorrow
They lined the tracks for miles never daring
to consider tomorrow
Over a thousand sad miles he traveled
and stopped at many towns
His casket was unloaded so many could
witness the nation's crown
Thousands wept in silence and bowed their
heads in shame
The black clouds enveloped hearts as they
looked for the souls to blame
He came for only such a time
as this
History told the story of how we would
always miss
His thoughts, his spirit, his ideas
carried high in the wings of hawks
All the way to Springfield and he laid to rest
a final last
Tears make us recall, such a bloody
past

Old Photographs and Wild Dreams

One way ticket from human nightmare
never wanted to go back home again
….......nothing there for me anymore
-except family
they don't care for me
wretched prison food still digesting in my gut
scars that won't heal
I didn't do it
….......really
No one believed me
the damned bus was full and was forced to buy a train ticket
hungry...can't sleep...three more hours
Locust Springs...nobody will hire me
no friends
bad memories and new ones will probably be the same
damn...damn...damn
momma will cry and say lots of things
daddy will be silent...cold eyed...grunt
brothers and sisters will act like nothing happened
in public
at home they will talk a blue streak
about me
...he looks hard....can't believe he's back...what's he going to do?
…he can't stay with us...nobody will hire him
Got up and bought black coffee
one cup...forty minutes the man said
cold sweat on my brow
shouldn't have drank the coffee
bad for nerves
maybe work construction...they don't care about this kind of shit
work my ass off and leave Locust Springs
I'm kidding myself...correction-- bull shitting myself
where would I go?
I'm going home

Old Photographs and Wild Dreams

Way back into yesterday, a long time ago
when rail men were kings and travel was slow
The big old engines ran on wood, fire and coal
folks would stare as the box cars would roll
Passengers too would hop a western ride
over the mountains along the blue tide
But the six one nine had the pride of the best
chugging up passes and rushing over the crest
The pure mountain air would sail through her load
waving at spruces until it came time to unload
Luxury berths served with elegant copper pots
whiskey bars around gamblers winning jack pots
Crowded with money bound for the coast
owning a ticket was a working man's boast
There came a bad winter with curtains of snow
the six one nine plowed steady as the inches did grow
Pushing the frozen barriers and climbing so high
past the tree line and almost touching the sky
But the mountain was heavy with God's white blanket
beautiful evening a mythological banquet
The avalanche broke loose and began to slide
pushing boulders downward to the engineer's pride
A snowy wall swept the train from the tracks
falling and tumbling splitting the cracks
Prayers too late went up the snow line
death was the day for the six one nine
Down in the wreckage buried in the deep
frozen wide eycd seemingly asleep
Gentlemen and ladies who never knew
when the moment had come for this rendezvous
Stories are told around the campfires
when nature triumphs over man's desires

Old Photographs and Wild Dreams

His mind wandered through the winding tracks that narrowed once they left Denver
doubts...hellacious doubts
The newspapers...the damn papers told of miners getting rich
millionaires by the dozen
gold plated lives
Instead there had been dozens going home along the way- dead broke- frozen in the
high Rockies
But here we sat...passing the Chalk Cliffs and heading up up up to the last leg of the trip
St Elmo
Spruce pine aspen and deer- elk too they say
Beginning to snow, but the conductor said it would be light, said we would all be drinking
in the saloon before dark
Bought a claim...back in Iowa-he swore it was a steal- I would be rich
Bought his tools and cases
Bought his dreams too
Doubts...hellacious doubts
His wife cried and begged- he tried to explain he weren't no farmer – no flatlander
His brothers would look after her...he would be sending money back soon lots of money
Gave her banking instructions
The cold in the rail car was unbelievable
was this all a dream? A miner's dream who had never swung a pick axe?
Night was falling as they entered the burg
St Elmo
It felt like it was only afternoon but the sun was gone
over Tin Cup pass
There's the hotel...small and lighted up
men in boots everywhere
Mules, horses, oxen, a few cows
wagons and buggies
A saloon whose lanterns lit the porch and seemed inviting
Unloaded and squeezed into a tiny bar
elk steak and potatoes along with cheap whiskey

God damn it got cold up here- no oxygen
but talk of nuggets, big ones – riches in their eyes
Talked with the man who will take him to the claim
lots of color he promised, easy pickings
Sleep came sparsely as he awaited the dawn and the promise of the color

Old Photographs and Wild Dreams

War is over and we are crushed
blackened fields and burnt bridges
dot the country side
death is everywhere
the smell of blood and the loss of hope
brings him to the place
where the trains used to run
now bombs have destroyed a way of life
twisted metal and silly looking parts of
passenger cars – split open – gashed into bits
miles of wreckage
what will become of all this metal carnage?
What were they feeling when they saw their bombs fall?
Happy? Sad? Giddy?
Such a waste! A millennium will pass and this junk will remain
a lesson
war
Walking among the horror
piles of rusty wheels – walls of box cars stacked
like jagged card decks
one remains almost intact
he peers inside
Dinning car – table cloths dirty but still on the job
curtains billowing in the accidental breeze
nearly dark – sounds from the western fringe
hobos
living off the wreckage
he sighs and then traipses off on the empty tracks
no fear of an engine coming tonight

Old Photographs and Wild Dreams

They named her the 4th and she was a beauty
she carried the lumber and that was her duty
Across the divide and down into old Denver
the 4th went anywhere the bosses would send her
Burning hot coal and out gunning the bandits
even in winter she seemed to understand it
Huffing and pushing at high altitude
her engine was strong – good was her mood
Loud was her whistle and clang went the bell
the 4th had the right juju – all did bode well
The men who drove her past the vast plains
boasted of her speed, her heart, her brains
Tons of Oregon lumber and steel from the north
even the big cities heard tales of the 4th
One day it happened, the brakes they did fail
off a steep corner and leaving the rails
Crashed in a canyon and there it did lay
parts of her body are there till this day
The stories still live and there never will be
a train like the 4th from sea to shinning sea
Her memory is written in many a royal court
a tear and smile to her, the mighty 4th!

Old Photographs and Wild Dreams

Across the Finnish landscape
　　feel the light air
Cross the station tracks
　　mount the steps
Train springs forward
　　right on time
Mountains of snow
　　steep divide
Clickity-clack
　　long darkness
Seemingly endless
　　tiny dot of light
Red, no...yellow
　　daylight again
Sunlight blazes and
　　the world rushes in
Frozen little cabins
　　darkness again
Forests of light green
　　stone arches
Ancient blue lakes
　　roads and few cars
Climbing up high
　　then down
Down, down, down
　　valleys so vast
Snow drifts that topple
　　darkness and wind
Metallic chang
　　faster speed
Clickity-clack
　　longer
Much longer darkness
　　COMPLETELY BLACK
Eternal void-like
　　mysterious fear
Station lights burn
　　night time sleep

Old Photographs and Wild Dreams

Heading west on a four o'clock train
rode all night through the cold Chicago rain
Restless sleep, if any at all
can't see the towns, just a wet wall
Handcuffed and watched, expecting the worst
silent copper not to converse
Wishing to God, to stay on this train
silent Sam, doesn't want the same
Knew I'd get pinched, guess it didn't matter
window watching the wet birds scatter
Hungry now, Sam doesn't answer
no one to help, folks died from a cancer
At least a smoke this tongueless monster
bill boards nice, forgetting the sponsor
Thinking of Gomer, his pet Lab
who will take him? Makes him more sad
Probably Pepper, the girlfriend, the pigeon
should have never trusted her type of religion
Regrets and hindsight, always around
wishing this bastard at least make a sound
How many years will the judge make a gift?
never met a soul, this cheerless, this stiff
Cuffs are aching bad, no chance in hell
will Sam emerge from his shell
I think I heard a whistle, a call for a stop
must be close, fewer rain drops
We're slowing down, Sam come alive
finally muttered "be there in five"
St Louis bound and here we stop
won't be long and in the noose I will drop

Old Photographs and Wild Dreams

Rolling in the mountains
    trails in the cold
Frosty air pushes up the collar
    pedaling through Alpine gold
Two wheeled wonder
    takes him to be free
Deeper in the woods
    quaking Aspen trees
Along the die cast journey
    encounter witches spell
Colors of the rainbow
    drinking at the wizard's well
Handle bar heaven
    a seat of leather brown
Speeding down the slopes
    quiet whirring sound
Moons of Jupiter rising
    back pack full of books
Bouncing through the rocks
    the trail's devilish hook
A time of year to listen,
    pause and behold
Hours on the beast
    hardly feel the cold
Muscles in the stomach
    tight with grinning teeth
Stopping at the trout stream
    lungs ache to breathe
Deeper in the day
    lying under a Spruce
Uncorked the bottle
    spooked a feeding moose
Chardonnay in the grass
    a mood it does employ
Red metal wonder
    far from city noise
Life on two wheels
    a way of growing old

No one around
  he never fit the mold

Old Photographs and Wild Dreams

Lying on his back in the grassy past of a day gone too wrong
he thinks...his mind wanders backward to
a time
simplicity and black and white
days on a bicycle seat
rusty chain and mornings

Before paranoia and adult miseries
he rides down a woody path toward a gurgling creek
splashing through muddy dips
not a care...sun burning hot
making scorched circles on his cheeks
the wind calls

Riding to school and leaving his Schwinn leaned
against the fence
no locks or worries
always there when school was over
home work and silent moments alone
thinking of wild forbidden dreams

"Why did I leave it behind?"
cars and sixteen came calling
beer and wrecks...back seat kissing
screeching tires...eight tracks
long back street drives
adulthood

Now I am older
(he acknowledges begrudgingly)
but longs for days alone
on a mountain trail
shoulder birds and a bike
long bumpy rides

Old Photographs and Wild Dreams

Iron gates opened and the boy had become a man

Prison days were over and the wasted times of sand

Friends were vanished and a chance at money too

Walking down a highway with different sizes of shoe

Washing dishes bought a meal, a beer and a cot

Saving nickels for a Flyer dominated all his thought

Six long months and summer came too slow

Free world lifesaving had the material dough

Bike in the window and down the road he sailed

No destination plotted he never thought to fail

Nights in the pines by a simple fire and meal

Sleeping under branches easy snoring steal

Sometimes the coppers chased him down the road

His kind of freedom threatened middle class abode

Over the mountain on a western route

Two wheels sent him to the streams of trout

On to the ocean and the piers that people love

Two wheels turning life and its 'most of'

Old Photographs and Wild Dreams

Denver cloudburst

    rusty chain

Soaked to the skin

    hung over brain

Parked and shivered

    old brick alley

Familiar jazz window

    'bout a gal called Sally'

Pedaled down Eighth

    corners flooded

Sedan out of nowhere

    comical but sudden

Pushed her hard

    both tires went flat

Found the java

    there I sat

Safe and dryer

    window gazed

Sheets of rain

Old Photographs and Wild Dreams

lightening blazed

Mountains in the distance

    blurred by the storm

Flecks of snow

    winter born

Piles of books

    known and unknown

Stories of desires

    under the stones

Thomas Wolfe speaks to me

    faded cover

Turn the page

    plot discover

Rains declined

    remarks toward the night

Pushing up Broadway

    faded street light

Old Photographs and Wild Dreams

Lying on a summer hammock...

looking at the scars
hard to remember
never forget others
painful

Lying on the fall leaves

scars on the ancient sycamore
healed nicely- others
dead
wonderful age

Lying on a winter bed

bicycle wreck
hurt!
bent teeth
bent wheels

Lying under a spring grove of trees

contemplating tomorrow
understanding more
dreaming to capacity
smiling at the past

Old Photographs and Wild Dreams

Webster says it's a human desire...to want what someone has
the Bible says it's a SIN, though I've never heard a single sermon
on the subject-
why?
Burglars must commit this act before they burgle
Adulterers must also engage in this vice before they 'adulterize'
Rich folk must love this word – but so do the poor
to want ...to desire...to long...to yearn
TO COVET!

Hobo just wanted a new bike-
he had an old one-
rusty-wobbly- laughing stock
broken seat and bald tires
not cool
NO MONEY!

Hobo didn't covet money-
or a job that belonged to
someone else- or a credit plan
with monthly payments
or charity from the mission
JUST A NEW BIKE!

So, he stole one from the store-
right in front of everyone-
no one chased him- thought he
just testing it out- he was not
he kept the bike and therefore-
HE NO LONGER COVETS!

Old Photographs and Wild Dreams

Happened again like it did years ago...middle of the night
dreams...heavy syrupy dreams with dark corners
strange faces- unknown places
I was- I think I was...
in a bar...a mountain bar
in the mountains- woody and taxidermy specimens on the walls
dark floors and loud music
smoky and in the dead of winter

Bikes- not motorcycles- not Harleys
bicycles...dozens of them
among the people
Happy- but excited with a purpose- they bounced
vibrated and danced among the drunk patrons
all different ages, sizes, and colors...
the bikes (I mean)
the drunks were about the same...
big, loud, hairy and generous...
always buying rounds

What does it mean? Hell-
if I know...but it happened again
and again and again...
maybe- it's heaven
for some- as for me...I was there
among the dancing bikes...drinking
madness it seemed- but deep down it felt good
really exquisite

So...maybe bikes go to heaven- and
they like to get together...
in bars...and drink...with humans
if so...when did this begin? Because bikes haven't
been around forever...if so-
Maybe all the happiness they brought to humans
caused this phenomenon
Heaven?

I look forward to another deep dream-
trip wired by a night of fellowship
and drinking- and a cornucopia of events-
from the day- followed by sleep surrounded
by city honking – or beach sounds-
or something else...

Old Photographs and Wild Dreams

An Okie in the nineteen thirties
   grandfather to me
Dustbowl memories
   he told the stories you could see
Plowing the Earth
   living off the land
Raised seven offspring
   his only definite plan
Looking into his eyes
   scanning Indian tales
Student of the Bible
   while lifting cotton bales
Loved old western black and whites
   to him they rang true
Worked hard behind a mule team
   hot days with skies of blue
Muscles in his arms
   authority on his voice
Spending days with him
   a time of veritable rejoice
Yes, he had problems
   and troubles not a few
Recalling years with him
   his shadow I still pursue
Dirt farmer with little education
   a man they did respect
His simple abode was always
   ample garden blessed
I think of him often
   because of the blood inside my heart
Sunny days with Poppa
   Stained forever in my art

Old Photographs and Wild Dreams

crazy abstract drawings – jagged hopelessness
lost love...jumping off cliffs – binges for days
blonde haired fallacies
motel days watching gray snow fall
fantasies of the unknown- impossible thought
waves
ugly faces
snow tire traces...strawberry wine- old poets passing
joints
mexicans drinking Jägermeister
cemetery memories...eating sandwiches in the sun
tiny motel room- watching movies on an ancient
television
classics
reading Whitman and Burroughs – next door
lovemaking noises
Rolling Stones Magazine...looking old in the
mirror
busted guitar – worthless to the pawn
broker
winter flu season
storm coming soon- holes in both boots – strawberry
wine
telephone call – bringing hope
hitch a ride to Old Denver
Jack's stomping grounds – Charlie
Brown's
tired
late night oil burning – crazy
thoughts
winter
wine
winter time

Old Photographs and Wild Dreams

A POET AND THE BEACH

Herman lived in a driftwood shack
alone and far from town
A province of tea and biscuits
isolated and hunkered down
Sitting by the shoreline
listening to the birds
Poems came a springing
in the wind they could be heard
Writing by the hundreds
Herman kept the books
He swore he couldn't sell them
they didn't have a hook
His words painted pictures
of ships sunk long ago
Mermaids and pirates
adventures with an evil glow
At night Herman waited
by a surplus lantern light
People would drift by him
and then continue out of sight
Talking held no pleasure
only the rhyming line
For years he listened and recorded
summers long and cold winter time
Herman died at last
deep in the ocean's wheels
Eternity he chants and visits
with the dolphins and the seals

Old Photographs and Wild Dreams

Junk sleep restlessness transporting the soul backwards

Amarillo...the seventies...early seventies

Colorado driving...almost dead tired

Hungry- have to stop – Big Red's Cafe

old concrete walls...faded paint...Dr Pepper circle

cracked glass door...strong smells...mushy bacon

burnt toast, eggs, ham...burnt...all of it

stomach revolts...but the will says "EAT"

counter stool...bad coffee...splintered cup

flies ride on the dusty ceiling fan

cowboy boots, hats, jeans, attitude

staring out the window...Colorado license plates

frowns – eggs arrive scrambled – not -

sunny side up – coffee cold – toast is ok

Big Red's is glad to see me pay and leave

Goodbye Amarillo! Goodbye sleep! Hello Tums!

Next stop – Chillicothe – population 707

Old Photographs and Wild Dreams

Hollow feelings from cold shoulder disappointment

...lightning fast rejection...the 405...fancy cars

problems

Escape floods the zone of the heat wave

...cracks on the sidewalk...mocking...vomit clumps

on the bus seat...cruel stares

rudeness

Run down Santa Monica Boulevard...snaking

the traffic...past the city life...toward the blessings

of the palms...rollerblading monks...Pacific calm

routine

Turn up the "1" and head north...Malibu...cool

shore breezes...blood pumps slower...beach...Beach Boys

sing in the light air...surf boards...fish cafe's

white houses...balconies...Harley's...sunshine

peace

Wednesdays are the best...no hump required...hilltop

views...magnetic pull toward the ocean...rocky wave

jets...dolphins pair up...perform...seals...elude

sunset hides the palms...high tide...birds scutter

back and forth...avoiding the waves

sandy home with a bottle...

Old Photographs and Wild Dreams

BARNEY'S (ON 66)

Barn like existence

depression era country shop

Racist Anthony muddled but

immortalized the license plates

Turtle Blues and R. Crumb

inspired by beer and chili

Cheap Thrills opened the doors

Joplin and Morrison, gone too soon

wooden beams home to orange

ghosts who look down on the living

Late night whiskey

Clark Gable with a frown

Jim and Jimi

drank on every stool

Judy Garland and Rita Hayworth

linger playing pool

Unique shaking karma

breakfast on the porch

Tarantino scribbling Pulp

Bukowski by the urinal

Janis' last stop

October dark night

poets wasting time

looking for words

Bartenders in a fight

may it last forever

Monroe sees Clara Bow

curtain opens daily

West Hollywood is the show

Old Photographs and Wild Dreams

The day was too long, office hours stretched
into a defining sadness
Home life was nil, except for Felix, a once missing
feline of madness
Resisted the bars, shops and molten traffic
line of clutter
Throat was silent from all the mindless words
the morons could utter
Comfort was urgent and the way was so
very close
Waited his turn on the bench 'till he was called
and arose
To a Roscoe table and to gaze at the colorful
food and choices
Chicken and waffles was the heavenly words
and the voices
Coffee was black with cream, waitress conversation
and sugar
She was friendly to boots and definitely a
physical hugger
Soon came the plate, the size of a coffee book
table
Fried chicken, waffles, butter and syrup
like out of a fable
He ate and he smiled, nodded and wiped
off his chin
Sat there groggy, listless, but content in
his skin
Roscoe's House will forever be the only
California cure to some
When that day from hell has dawned and your
mind is truly numb
Chicken and waffles, what an odd couple
to be found
Don't knock it 'till you tried it, and there
you'll be bound

Old Photographs and Wild Dreams

True back pages...finding the "you" and who that is-

discovery – words – words together

rhymes?

lost love...

Diedrich's Coffee Shop (on 12th) journaling

Penn's Perk (poems)

birthing a western soul … old brick four stories and cold snow days

finding a home (temporary) on a gray second floor

Logan Street address...balcony on 11th...suits and freaks below

constantly

Cafe Netherworld – Park Tavern

candle nights...no television ...no friends

endless soul wool gathering ...mountains to the west

The Fort -

Starry Night...Muggz...Bean Cycle

Trailhead Tavern....Josh...Graham

Finding that place...the soft walls of zen where writing springs...

People...no people

bicycles on the curb – frozen

Old Photographs and Wild Dreams

Lonely and depressed = stone cold poems...breaking down old patterns

that don't work- no longer fits

writer everyday ...every day ...find that "cave" - that
"write place"

Look! And canoe around inside the mind...travel

Look!

Talk!

Listen

Old Photographs and Wild Dreams

Wake up from a North Hollywood sun

then a California shower followed by a Red Line run

Trample down the sleepy Boulevard and all that ungodly

to those smiling faces at Cafe Audrey

Strong black java and a free wifi world

cozy cushioned corner and let the mind whirl

Every day was golden then, even the tawdry

Longing for days at Cafe Audrey

Named for the legend by a woman called Dottie

A home for writers, actors and some of the naughty

Larry, the brewmaster, a friend at the "Audrey"

Bob played the piano for a free cup of coffee

Screenplays about broken hearts made some days a bit foggy

Sometimes, while washing away washing the hangover groggy

I think of those days at Cafe Audrey

strong impressions and even stronger coffee

Her image is still there, but the rest is in the wind

My memory of her is for a long lost friend

The days I spent there made me feel like "somebody"

So, I'll raise a glass to her memory: Cafe Audrey

Old Photographs and Wild Dreams

Five orange letters, a beacon in the night

wasted California evening, needed relief from a fight

Hot blacktop traffic, LA neon haze

palms on the corner, Chevy's in a maze

Parked and gave my name, table soon arrived

ordered ham and eggs, Raymond Chandler style

Big glass windows, inside the busy bees worked

stirred black coffee, with a shiny old fork

In ten the chow was here, waitress with a smile

wolfed down the paradise, had to last many a mile

Love was in the air, comfort in the storm

always going back, that corner lot for Norm's

Old Photographs and Wild Dreams

I love days at the park
Days of warm sunshine feelings
Freedom to enjoy life with my girlfriend
Shopping separately for a perfect afternoon
Loading and unloading the caravan supplies we take
Table and chairs, wine and food, guitar and books to read
Setting up to claim our spot under old trees that are slowly dying
From a long California drought but still shades us with the life it still has
Songs & fire cooked steaks as we share our hearts and souls in the open air
I love days at the park

Old Photographs and Wild Dreams

Waking before dawn into a poor life he welcomes

    reporting to a rickety shack from a signal that beckons

Stacked with fruit left from his brother and neighbor

    picked in the starlight with sweaty brown labor

Pineapples are lined up like soldiers in summer

    oranges on the corners, in their beauty and wonder

Mangoes that are fresh, soft and so juicy

    bananas grown local, with flavor that suits you

He doesn't wait long and they stop and they gander

    buying his wares that daily seem grander

As the evening steals the light, he must close the stand

    Never worrying as he leaves it unmanned

An honest living, the salt of the earth

    He loves his job and knows his worth

Old Photographs and Wild Dreams

VENTURA

ventura
tacos on the pier
beach squirrels scouting the tides
Cafe Fiore pouring liquid dreams afternoons
Sunday morning coffee enjoying empty streets for hours
sitting on the pier as fishermen launch their bait
staring at water life between the waves
Channel Islands Ferry
101 white noise
ventura

Old Photographs and Wild Dreams

Shiny Packards find a place and park
    Men in fedoras order bourbon on a lark
War is over and the factories are running
    Over in the corner, an old man is humming
Beer and whiskey, a penny for a bartender's thoughts
    Neon signs, blinking low watts
Belmont Tavern opens early for the masses
    Truman's on the headlines, adjusting his glasses
Brick and mortar pantheon, offering eclectic tastes
    Water closet toilet, mirror to the waist
Beer for a quarter, cigars for a dime
    Politics and religion, considered a crime
Belmont Street alley cats, know all the secrets here
    Cold winter evenings, "open" sign massages the air
Closed in the '80's, when the jobs went south
    Memories of her legend, only from a drunkard's mouth
Poetry for a time, dance hall magic
    When she died, life became more tragic

Old Photographs and Wild Dreams

Old brick monolith...home to Chief Two Moons
Under the mountain shadows...Pike's Peak nephew
Golden beer ale...made from Colorado agua
Clean glass windows...hiding late night secrets
Always a crowd...bar stool neighborhood
Three story wonder...relief from the steep trail
Business men meeting girlfriends ...naughty
Last call in the winter...freezing silent air
Sunday morning eggs...magical bloody marys
Pool and billiards...talk about the week
Beer tastes better...made on the block
Coco's Ranch...cousin to Shady Nasty
Skippy must be German...Livonia is his lover
Two Headed Dog...last of the evening
Phantom is a monument...beer gods of the Rockies

Old Photographs and Wild Dreams

A while ago, or was it just the other day?

   An old friend of mine....had something he wanted to say

We decided to meet, and it was kind of late

   -he told me of a funky little place on eighth

The bar was kind of crowded – but somehow I got a drink

   My friend was late arriving...gave me time to think

The walls held lighted candles, music felt old and deep

   ...my insides churned with lightening, days away from sleep

My friend knew the people, all smiles and teeth

   In the back some hipsters danced, a few began to leap

The old fat idol winked at me and urged me toward the fun

   ...his eastern ways intrigued me, his face never saw the sun

On the roof, the stars of Denver shone brightly through the clouds

   Many things dawned on me, the naked and the proud

Winter, spring, and summer, the changes were so quick

   the art of life came alive – along those streets of brick

My friends were so many, a few were kind of frumpy

   A chapter of my life, where the Buddha was so funky

Old Photographs and Wild Dreams

Over a ragged hill and down a cactus ravine

    Big Red and Boxcar Shorty ran through the thick smoke screen

Hard tack miles without sleep up the mountain pass

    Winter fires were burning through the window glass

Small burg nestled by the simple and the good

    The pair that came upon them, they never understood

Holding court, Red and Shorty drank and spilled much blood

    What sort of humans drove life even from the tree's bud?

Evil had arrived and drove the town to dust

    Everything shiny, had now began to rust

Is this just a fable, or a lie that people tell?

    Actually, this is America, a modern living hell

Old Photographs and Wild Dreams

western establishment awash in cheap liquor- bad sorts linger
early and late
smelly floors and dirty windows as cold wind blows- warm beer
most days
seedy outlook on a stage of old guitars – bar stools broken and -
hearts and minds
loudmouth brings bad news and shaky credit – fists collide and blood -
spurts
whiskey thoughts attract red lip stick and short skirts – lusty old -
criminals
neon dancing crowd the Saturday night lovers intent -
back seat humping
beer label virgins peel away everything mothers taught – in
Sunday School
sermons from the bartender he learned from the sport's section -
today's paper
tears and smiles boosted by opening a new bottle as a stranger -
walks inside
all these ingredients churn and bake into a beat poetry -
pie
Presidents and Roman Emperors never knew as much insight -
as the local poet

Old Photographs and Wild Dreams

Stranger sauntered inside on a hot summer eve

The other folks had paid their tab and started their leave

He ordered a beer and shot with a grin

Waited in silence, tattoos on his skin

He drank and stated my name is "Jones"

The bartender shook hands, who was called Malone

In that tavern, that warm afternoon pleasure

Jones spun a tail of adventure and treasure

The old brick walls and blonde wood bar

Seemed to laugh and shake, breaking some jars

Malone, he just listened, poured and smiled

Out the window rolled a hearse with too many miles

Pirates and dragons, were all in his life

Divorces and cheating left Jones with no wife

He hoped that in Denver, his luck would change

Maybe another wedding for a man who seemed so strange

In an hour or two, the crowd squeezed along the rail

Happy hour and work stories, and how some always fail

Night birds call out and they sing a tune

How Jones and his stories, happened that warm afternoon

Old Photographs and Wild Dreams

Thirty-two counties and thirty-two friends
    Irish legends every one of them

A pot of pure gold and an Irish grin
    Step forth and enjoy the fun and sin

The walls tell the stories, ghosts whispering true
    Guinness in the pint glass and Jameson not a few

Patrick is the Lord, lift up his banner
    Associate with his angels and their heavenly manner

A well-worn stage where music is born and played so well
    Songs of a green homeland, a shepherd rings his bell

The bar is a friend to all who garnish a stool
    To doubt or not believe this, why only a fool

St Patrick's Day and Christmas, the ground swells and shakes
    Funerals and birthdays, the love they do make

A star in the Almighty's sky, the devil would agree
    A long, long way from Claire, but its citizens you can see

Old Photographs and Wild Dreams

Up toward the clouds

Pike's Peak climb

Sat his brick kingdom

Orange chairs and cold beer

Bronco fever pitch gambling

Car salesmen and floozies

Hooks and hopeless romantics

Oriental smile and handshake

Hot wings and fries

Tears and a shoulder to cry on

Cold mountain evenings

Friendship bonds that still hold

Happiness to the unknowing

Discovery of an inner self

Reliable good times

Thank you my friend

Old Photographs and Wild Dreams

ENDSVILLE CIRCUS BAR

Adopted home of Hippie Electrum's stories

    Fictional beach dive bar south of Venice

California that is...

Winter hangout of circus folk- clowns, and other misfits

    Who long for spirits

The kind you find in a bottle that is...

Made of weathered gray wood, large and spacious

    Well stocked and lots of other stuff

Like food that is...

Circus folk shepherd the weak, the misfits,

    They show kindness to strangers

And buy them drinks that is...

Endsville is the end of the line

    the barren beach colony

And no rules that is...

Bohemia at its best

    Writers and bums, poets and dancers

The topless kind that is...

Weird and weirder are draped all over walls

Houdini's ghost drinks there sometimes

with Emmett and Barnum

Kelly and PT that is...

Oh you should go and see

Become a believer

A true one that is...

Old Photographs and Wild Dreams

TRAILHEAD BLUES

Alpine mornings on Mountain Avenue

Doors wide open
Drinkers social hours
Do gooders nightmare
Drunken happiness

Afternoons at the Fort

On everyone's mind
Out door porch smoking
Opera to the lonely and outcasts
Orthodoxy to native souls

Evenings off College

Lights down the avenue
Lots of assorted bicycles
Lingering day drinkers
Leasing Paradise

Sundays at the Head

Angel winged games
Anthems of cheap booze
Amusement away from reality
Antipathy toward social rules

Old Photographs and Wild Dreams

Ticking tock clocks

Four pm magical change in North Hollywood life
First in the door gets the coveted booth perches
Fandango blender noises mute the conversations
Five dive liquor drinks warm the body

Behind the bar

Knowledge of the unknown ingredients
Kilowatts burn the potions together
Kamikaze spirits labor in the juices
Kaleidoscope colors spin inside the glasses

Out in the booths

Secrets are spilled
Screenplays are hatched and reborn
Souls grow and befriend
Splashes on insanity and goodness

Away from the Hut

Cold turkey withdrawal
Complete plans are sketched
Counting the hours
Conspiracies are followed on Facebook

Old Photographs and Wild Dreams

Some days...I awaken to still being

a Baker Street boy

A Texas fog of childhood

memories

Old run-down house...slowly remodeled

basement shared with brother David

Tree house construction...injuries

paper route days

Rock and roll came to town

Dallas concert

Shot guns by the railroad tracks

black bass dinners

Cousins next door...funny fence stories

Thanksgiving

Growing pains...Daniel's asthma pump

James playing under the Christmas tree

Transformative time in our childhood....personalities

...likes and dislikes...longing again for Amsden

Mrs. Cooke's History and trips to Colorado

Funerals to remember and riding the bus

Bicycle Saturdays at the Rialto...six Pepsi caps

Mowing grass at Tanglewood...one dollar per hour

Fifty hours a week....chiggers all over...sulfur tablets

Hot summers and cold winters...sleet

Learning to drive...driver's ed...license

Thinking and planning...dreams

Memories of Baker Street...boys

Old Photographs and Wild Dreams

End of the long road and the beginning of the fork

Finding poetic lines along with trips to New York

Daily coffee made life more like art

Penn's Perk birthed writing from the heart

Another lifetime, swallowed up and gone

New words and ideas suddenly spawned

Denver days and Colorado nights

Inward soul searching switched forward the lights

Poor rice and beans, a pauper's lot

Walking old sidewalks, Western Soul was brought

Depression ugliness and endless doubt

Coming to an end, just wanted out

That never came, but more humble learning

Texas minutes, Denver yearning

Bread and butter, never found home again

Foundation dried at 11th & Logan

Old Photographs and Wild Dreams

Back when time was young and the mountains were so large
      Stores closed at 5 pm
      Church was life et al.
      Deep snow winters
      75 dollars per week
Love from the heart on dirt streets and lead mines
      St Elmo skiing
      First trip to Denver
      Matchless Mine stories
      Small town politics
Deer hunting on the Blue River
      Long quiet treks alone
      Heart quaking at the sight
      Winter meat atop the station wagon
      Ruining the dinning table
Prayer meetings that lasted forever
      True religion
      Devoid of politics
      Frontier faith
      Love for God
Chain saw days for wood in the mountains
      Cold nights around a fire
      Cedar street smells good
      Little boys at Christmas
      Meals with friends
Life was good and seemed to last
      Lessons learned
      Chapters turned
      Past is past
      Memories still burn

Old Photographs and Wild Dreams

Old orange sun moving slowly across deserts palms and houses

the settles on a ribbon of blacktop and imagination arouses

Up the California coast as it winds, twists and climbs

hairpin corners that suddenly slam so blind

The ONE holds a history of movie stars, poets and workers

past cauliflower fields and pools of writhing fish that murmur

Mudslides and fires are just a normal day of travel

vacationers simply make the drive to relax and unravel

Rocky coastline beauty makes the way a little slower

tensions of the mind are lost as the temps start to lower

Palmy beaches serving surfers and nightly campfire pleasure

ghosts of old pirates seeking fame, fortune and treasure

Bumps and cures and time to drive ONE mile

grumpy middle age men look out and start a rare smile

Gaze fully at Oxnard, Lompoc, San Luis Obispo's charms

Monterey, Santa Cruz, Santa Rosa's farms

Up north lies Mendocino, Westport and the end of the line

ONE is a creature unequaled, a wonder of our time

Steep mountains, rocky blue ocean, and dolphins' delight

A California creature: Steinbeck, Kerouac, and God's starlight

Old Photographs and Wild Dreams

I dreamed of old Colfax last night...Majestic Denver's artery
                              night time headlights
                              Catholic church crowds
                              hookers in dark alleys
                              drugs in little bags passed
Capitol Hill's best/worst friend that never changes or gives a second
chance
                              cornucopia of needs being sold
                              music from the Fillmore
                              bars that seem to not close
                              artists, true artists that paint
A vein shoots off into museums, night clubs, Broadway and government
                              blues and yellows
                              funky beat and smoke
                              blue collar workers
                              automobile salesmen
Hearts rest easy along its traffic behind large old Victorians and mansions
                              poor beg for money
                              homeless freeze in the parks
                              girls trick for dope and food
                              unemployed seek minimum wage
From the eastern plains to the mountain gateways
                              cars move swiftly
                              Colorado colors blaze with hope
                              snow falls heavy on all
                              angels tend their flock

Old Photographs and Wild Dreams

Orange trees laden with heavy fruit and green lawns freshly mowed

North Hollywood central with California life that never closes

Traffic from the canyons and deserts way beyond

Down and outers weeping openly of the items they have pawned

Mom and Pop stores thrive and serve the unlikely

Bars and ritzy condos serve the high and mighty

A stone's throw from Malibu and the oceans over the hills

The busy street pulses and bends to an ancient will

Wrought iron gates and house parties, loud on Saturday nights

Seven Eleven hangers sometimes deal and fight

Car washes aplenty, banks and taco trucks bake in the hot sun

Crossing Van Nuys and Sepulveda, after hard work is done

The Metro runs sporadic, and the seats stay pretty full

Green lawns in winter months, resists the colder pull

My first lesson in California life and change

An Oxnard house with strangers, became my home on the range

Walking the long blocks and finding how they were

Looking back there now, all seems to be a blur

The memories are all good, found true love and happiness

Oxnard street for those who understand, a poem of timelessness

Old Photographs and Wild Dreams

Sitting from a Starbucks perch at Highland, I see early morning
tourists gather with their foreign money to gasp at the palms and
the view of the sign

Yawning from a Starbucks perch at Highland, I hear the drone of
from The Boulevard, cruising down the Stars of the sidewalk, some
are locals making their way to work

Getting a second cup, I think of the years I have spent in this
neighborhood,
loving, despising, feeling the weird became normal at some point. What a
wonder to folks from Oklahoma, or Yokahama

Starbucks is crowded so I walk down The Boulevard, recalling the famous
I
seen, but mainly the infamous, known only to a few, but true Hollywood
treasures
that lived on the fringe

Bodegas selling tee shirts and hucksters selling tours, nod at me, don't
hassle me,
know I am a local, a fixture for at least a long chapter in my life. I hate/
love the
damn street, depending on the day

A walk down The Boulevard today brought Kenneth Anger gliding by, he
nodded a
and smiled an ancient Aleister Crowley toothy grin and disappeared up
Whitley to his
lair. (Always a good sign)

I was thinking about the Mayor and when I first came here. He was my
brother, oddly
teacher who showed me the greatness of just still being alive. Damn, I
miss him. His ghost
still haunts The Boulevard

I developed a real dislike for tourists and their rude behavior. But deep down, under all this crap and occasional ugliness, there lies the DNA of storytelling that changed our childhood and gave us a golden dream

Old Photographs and Wild Dreams

I remember Denison in its heyday...and
the intense excitement on Christmas mornings

Golden Rule School days- fresh wax on the wood floors

I remember Denison in its heyday...and
waiting for endless Katy rail cars to pass as
the signal rang loud

Burns Runs summers – Mrs. Cooke's eight grade
History class

I remember Denison in its heyday...when
all the factories were running

Dragging Main on Friday nights- chrome
engines gunning

I remember Denison in its heyday...when eight
tracks and miniskirts came to town

My first encounter with The Beatles- and learning
their songs

I remember Denison in its heyday...when
all the stores were open (and the barbershops)

I remember Watson's...and McDaniel Junior High School
and Saturdays at the Rialto

I remember the Safeway plant...where my daddy used to
work

Driving down Armstrong Avenue and buying gas for twenty-five
cents

I remember Sundays and eating Ashburns Ice Cream

Bomb shelter drills...polio sugar cubes

Long summer dreams

I remember Sid Maples and my first good guitar

Fishing in the winter

Heading to Dallas that seemed so far away

I remember the first time I fell in love there...
and smaller clothes fit me

I remember Denison in its heyday and when I wanted
to leave and explore more of the world

But looking backward brings a sweet feeling and an appreciation
for its hold on me then

Old Photographs and Wild Dreams

ROLLING DOWN THE ROAD

Arizona highway on a hot August night

Indians selling fireworks, liquor store on sight

Hitching with migrant pickers, weary and alone

Looking forward to the night, resting heavy bones

Stopping for a beer, tacos and the law

Speaking the local lingo, hating the steely claw

Neon dance hall down an alley of poverty dust

The women were all fleshy and fortunes had gone bust

Lying through my teeth and always expecting the worst

Gorging on a greasy special and slaking an aching thirst

The lady she was taken and so were all the doors

Brown fists on my face and my ass on the floor

Jumping through a too small window and running very fast

Here comes the migrant truck and all my troubles passed

Seventeen of us spread out on the spacious metal bed

Smoking the night reefer and not a word was said

Morning seems so distant and tired sweaty bodies drift off

Snoring then farting, enduring an old man's cough

The orange sun comes a walking so cool and very new

Stopping at a market, awning stripes of red and blue

Sipping on black coffee and the promised mirage of work

We roll down the block as the motor starts to jerk

Bound for California and the mountains look so far

Bouncing down the black top being passed by all the cars

Napping on a gas can, ignoring the smelly load

Me and my amigos, rolling down the road

Old Photographs and Wild Dreams

NOTHING TO WRITE ABOUT

once I was a number, just a digit, meaningless and standing in
a straight line obeying all the rules no matter how absurd

once I cried alone in the dark feeling sorry for myself and making
excuses for the brutality of others

once I saw glittering riches of others and decided to get some,
a little, all of it, to be like "them"

once I heard preachers telling me to fear, to change, to go to hell,
to cut my hair, buy new clothes

but this was nothing to write about...

there was a time when I was unhappy, failing to please anyone
no matter how hard I tried

there was a time when I worked all day and night was still told
I was worthless, no good

there was a time I was confused by what I saw in the mirror,
afraid of what was in my heart, my mind

there was a time I wanted to do many things but stood on the shore
watching ships sail away

but this was nothing to write about...

I remember when my tongue held evil words frolicking in the bigotry
of those dullards around me

I remember when my ears heard the drone of constant discouragement
and being crushed under its wheels

I remember when life seemed so long, so dull, so hard, and all I could
see was an endless pavement marked by stripes

I remember when I doubted truth itself and almost drowned in that deep well of dispair

but that was nothing to write about...

but then I saw and remembered so clearly...

when my childish fingers wrote letters to Washington, challenging war,

murder, and death

when I first saw Easy Rider and my eyes were opened and my heart became brave for the first time

when I first held a baseball and liked the way it felt, and then got a base hit and ran to first

when I heard the Beatles, the Rolling Stones, Jimi Hendrix, the Grateful Dead,
and Bob Dylan

when I discovered girls

and that was something to write about...

Old Photographs and Wild Dreams

Sitting in a deep December Starbucks trance
                        Holding secrets
                        Voices from the past
                        Things his mother said
                        No one wants to hear them

Friends around him buy drinks and slap his back
                        liquor eased the pain
                        smile in the mirror
                        fake feelings gone tomorrow
                        workers around him puzzling

Walking around a winter lake
                        He watches ducks navigate the shore
                        Wind whispers lies
                        Questions arise and fly away
                        Soul searching doesn't aid

Slouching on a court bench with faceless others
                        cold marble floors
                        old hardwood benches
                        stunned to be here
                        Judge calls his name

Stepping along a summer cemetery
                        Familiar names
                        Wakes attended
                        Names and dates
                        Nothing else

Killing days in a public library
>   perusing old phone books
>   begging to become lost
>   wilderness of words
>   avoiding the homeless

One day it stopped raining
>   Secrets uncovered
>   Sun shone brightly
>   Pain eased
>   Better days

Old Photographs and Wild Dreams

Gustavo drove his '48 Chevrolet coupe'

to the shipyards and then home to stay

On the trip home he stopped at Monroe's Bar

that lay across from a wrecked trolley car

A beer and a shot then to see man called "Mitch"

in the corner a copper was indulging a snitch

Mitch was a bookie and built like a bull

Gustavo loved the ponies by the urge of a gambling pull

Losing money he never explained to his lovely wife

to others he seemed to enjoy an American life

She would cook, wash and sew all of his clothes

he must have loved her once, now it didn't show

When he never came home, she began to worry

called the police and a Sergeant named Murray

Murray took the report and went back to his paper

Gustavo lay deep in the harbor, killed by murderous labor

Justice avoided and bad men in their dark glory

Gustavo's family suffered greatly, what a sad story

Old Photographs and Wild Dreams

SECRET HERO

Third, forth, and fifth graders all played on the same
dusty grounds- bullies proliferated and busted a few
mouths as they held a reign a fear & terror- one day
a new boy moved to town & was sent to this gladiator
hell for kids- I think his name was Tony- they started
calling his names like "phony baloney" & "tony the
pony" & "Tony Macaroni"- he didn't like it- not one
bit- but Tony wasn't a big kid- small or average I guess
but his uncle was a boxer- like a real honest to God
boxer- nobody knew that- Tony waited until after school
& and followed the biggest bully across the street- and
beat the living shit out of him- broke his jaw- Tony got
in trouble – big time- kicked him out of school- he came
back a few weeks later- the bullies were afraid of him- so
I guess they weren't bullies anymore-

Old Photographs and Wild Dreams

ELEPHANT HERD PHOBIA

Fear drove him crazy- couldn't cipher life
correctly

Living among the suits- inferior to them
directly

They loomed so large, all knowing-
smug smiles so ugly

He was just a worker bee, mediocrely competing
so bugsy

Piles of paperwork, afraid to take a break-
even a small one

His heart was weak and his compelling anger-
stayed mum

To live in fear inside those giant prison walls-
death was coming soon

One day he resisted the bulls and caught hell-
they fired him before noon

On the street he wandered and felt a lighter step-
no more phobias or daily crap

He lives free to day and wears a stylish, well made-
English flat hat

Old Photographs and Wild Dreams

TAYLOR MEAD

Several years ago I was privileged to meet
one of the last living beat poets in New York.
Taylor was still performing on Friday nights
at The Bowery Poetry Club and was reading
from his latest book "Taylor Mead, a Simple
Country Girl". He told stories of his life and
a few about Kerouac and life in San Francisco.
Taylor appeared in some of Andy Warhol's
underground films. When I saw him, he was
featured in "Coffee and Cigarettes". Born into
a wealthy family, his father got him a job on
the Chicago Stock Exchange, Taylor knew he
was not cut out for a conventional life. He
complained that night "I was raised by maids, no
one is more indifferent." After reading "On The Road"
he quit his job in Chicago and set out for San
Francisco. There are tales of him standing naked
on the bar at Vesuvio in North Beach, reading pages
from OTR aloud. The night I talked to him, his arm
was in a brace, having fallen down the steps to his
apartment, in a drunken haze, after celebrating his
84th birthday with friends. The friends (who were also
drunk) helped him inside and laid him on the pile of
bubble wrap at the foot of the Christmas tree. The
following morning he called 911 to fix the busted
arm. I can still remember the stories he told of being
in Rome in the 60's with Clint Eastwood and a host
of others who were exploring the world and their
talent. This book would not be the same unless I had
encountered this wonderful poet.

Old Photographs and Wild Dreams

Roland was fearless and never seemed tired- he loved his
wife and their five little kids- he worked at a factory that
made blue jeans and got a discount on them at Christmas
and sometimes in the summer- he was faithful to her
although she slowly withdrew from him because he wouldn't
seek a promotion or take them on a cross country vacation like
Chevy Chase did- he still worked forty hours a week and some
times on the weekend- he went with her to church and to visit
her parents who loathed him and said so right in front of him-
Roland like to watch baseball games on television and eat salt
and vinegar potato chips which his wife detested and told their
neighbors- he liked to fish but stayed home to make sure the lawn
was cut and the cars were freshly washed- he liked to have a beer
but his wife frowned on the idea and complained she was gaining
weight and somehow was his fault- his children said they loved
him and he took comfort in that thought- one rainy day on a
lonely trip to the grocery store he spied a man with a flat tire
and no spare tire- Roland stopped to help the man- he got wet just
like the man did and drove him to a tire store to buy a spare tire- on
the way back Roland felt free and easy talking to this grateful stranger
and blurted out "I always wanted to be a pirate-" the stranger just
laughed and said he did too-they changed the flat as the rain came
harder and saw a bar across the street- since Roland wouldn't accept
money he agreed to have a beer with the stranger and they sipped
Hamm's inside a dark wooden tavern and watched rain fall
through the thick glass and kept right on talking – before long Roland
found himself interested in what the stranger was saying and where he
was headed- Las Vegas- after the right amount of whiskey Roland
left his car in the rain by the bar and started for Las Vegas with his new
friend who come to find out was named Harold- Roland took turns driving
all night as they talked of pirates, baseball, potato chips, beer, church
and women- the sun came up and Roland chuckled – I'm supposed to
be going to work right now-

Old Photographs and Wild Dreams

Hollywood night streaming movies
from a time

Detectives sweating in summer,
always solving the crime

Third floor open window and
lights of a rooftop party

Sweet Caroline blasting from a wedding
sweet and artsy

Beer and whiskey another slice of
Trader Joe's pizza

Criminal in the courtroom suddenly
has amnesia

All the years in this hundred year
old room

Times sometimes bleak so it felt
like a tomb

Over time the history and events
got so much better

No longer trips to Wilcox just
to post a letter

The wedding gets louder and
sleep fairies have arrived

Dream ships commence launching-
time for a deep dive

Old Photographs and Wild Dreams

North Beach anchor of poetry and anarchy-bar to the rebel,
the thinker, the non-conformist, the pervert, the kind, the questioner,
the iron worker, the lawyer on his way to jail, the reader, the
hoarder, the alcoholic, the desperate artist, the fisherman, the lost,
the found

Neighbor to the Chinese, a metaphor to the masses, the walls so
lovely and ghostly...serving a purpose without the Americas- hell
the entire world would be devoid- poets, rebel writers, thinkers, readers,
the libertine- need a place- a home- not secluded in a damp cave- but
rubbing alcohol glowing shoulders with other who are like minded-
without
Vesuvio the world would not be the world

With its green and yellow coat to welcome you up the steps and bam!
You know this is different- past lights of Steam Beer and up those stairs
spiraling to a different place- out the window I see Ginsberg smoking a
joint with Dylan- Kerouac is walking toward them- they turn sharply into
City Lights to see what old Ferlinghetti is up to- paradise! Through the
window
you smell the bay and Fisherman's Wharf

May it always last- never torn down- others may perish but this Frisco
jewell
cannot be duplicated- never imitated...I am glad I was alive during the Age
of Vesuvio

Old Photographs and Wild Dreams

Lost in Value Forrest he wandered down a rocky trail
Words colliding through a word stream then a storm of hail

Managing to break free of cobwebs from a frightened spider
He came upon a colored canyon that seemed to grow wider

Thirsty and alone he wept, hungry and crestfallen
He knelt to pray and then he heard someone calling

His name rang from the canyon air and he jumped to see
Lizards scattered frightened and then the sting of a bee

Far out in the desert floor as the sun began to close
A group of men were approaching in a light of colored rose

Indians he thought in a canyon named Free and Wild
Dark skinned and painted being led by a little child

Dressed in feathers, buckskin and the like
The man smiled at them afraid they might want to strike

He waved at them but they only stared and kept upon their march
They stopped when they reached him with expression in an arch

He tried to speak and the words they came, never understood
The group of men also spoke with words of burning wood

Troubled and anxious he wanted to convey he came in peace
The Indians thought he was an enemy but had to make sure at least

An hour they struggled and even used their hands
Finally they both gave up and decided to take a stand

In the Valley of Honesty and down in the Canyon of Free and Wild
There lies a grave where red rocks are scattered and piled

A cross roads of trouble that need not have occurred
If only someone had understood words

Old Photographs and Wild Dreams

Winding my way up Laurel Canyon
past the store where the creatures meet

Evening traffic was light and I hung a
left on Mulholland without missing a beat

Whizzing past tree lanes and low mansions
over in the hidden dark

Sunset at dusk caught my heart so I found
a narrow pullout and decided to stay and park

Panoramic magic mixed with hardwood smoke
from a gated fireplace

Reached under the seat for a silver flask of bourbon
and let the radio volume race

An hour later, when the flask was dry, I closed
my eyes and felt the pace of this Hollywood road

A wolf howled, but it must be a coyote I thought,
but his spirit seeds were sowed

In my mind's eye Hollywood ghosts glided by and
gave greetings from another world

Bette Davis was curled up next to Jim Morrison in a
convertible like she was his girl

Mickey Rooney smoked a Cuban and was chatting
with W C Fields in a Roadster 44

The Marx Brothers zoomed by laughing being driven
by the drummer of The Doors

Alone in a Cadillac, Clark Gable slowed to gaze at me,
and then was gone with the wind

Old Photographs and Wild Dreams

James Dean and John Wayne looked like hungry wolves
prowling for a new den

On and on they came by me until the morning light
gradually woke me from this trance

Another starless night on Mulholland, as I return back
into the Valley, from an endless Hollywood dance

Old Photographs and Wild Dreams

He came from Ohio I think, a long time ago

Drove a truck for a while and then started selling blow

His girlfriend ratted him out, or that's what he thought

A stint in the clink, and eventually freedom he sought

I met him in a bar, an offbeat Hollywood joint

He had his own stool and made his own points

He welcomed me to the club and became a close friend

After six months he felt like he was my kin

A year younger in fact, we celebrated the same day

He hustled hard to pay his own way

Sleeping on the steps where they transferred the mail

No bank account, car or phone, there was a time he rode the rails

Don knew Hollywood, every mean street and painted door

Jägermeister got the best of him, nearly killed his core

He finally got clean, healthy, a job and a home

I still saw him on the streets where he was so known

His smile and wave made me cross the way and give a hug

The last time I saw him was by a Vine street fire plug

He seemed fine and promised a time for coffee and such

A month later he died and the news was so rough

I couldn't understand why or reason for his leaving

I miss the Old Mayor and I guess I'm still grieving

Old Photographs and Wild Dreams

ERNEST HESBY

He was first known as the new guy or new man
not Ernest, the new man
He moved to the little burg and worked at a paint and body outfit
we were told
The Tavern is where everybody met, drank, talked, etc.
that's where new man came
Newman sat on the regular stools and made friends with Carl
the bartender
They both liked the Packers and talked about them all the time
we never understood
Carl introduced newman to Ernest and newman became infatuated with
his stories
Ernest Hesby came every day at 4 and left at 6 or 630
give or take
Ernest drank PBR and read the newspapers that sat on the bar
after that he engaged in conversations
Newman hurried after work to make it to The Tavern in time to get a stool
next to Ernest, or close by
On days he had to work late, he still traveled there to find out what
Ernest was up to, what new stories he told
There was one time when Newman was off early and he was so happy
when he got there tourists or something had flooded the bar – no Ernest
The patrons of The Tavern had long ago given up whether the stories were
true or not
They were just so good and they seemed to get better each time he told
them to a new man – like Newman
Ernest was in his eighties when Newman came to meet him and instantly
recognized he was an enigma
Hesby would frequently get drunk and quote both Dylans- he claimed to
have met him- Bob, not Thomas
Hesby lived in a little cabin outside of town, down by the creek
said to have built all of it
He favored The Grateful Dead and big band music in his truck
always drove a new truck
He was certainly an enigma but more than that he seemed to have done
a little bit of everything
There was a certain air about him- an anticipation of something

extraordinary
he had enough money but wasn't arrogant
Said he was from the south and the old ways they had down there
his daddy worked in the rose fields of East Texas
His mother was in some of his stories and a few brothers and a sister
most not in a good way
Ernest Hesby was a hero to The Tavern and to many of strangers who had
met him
especially Newman

ERNEST HESBY

part two

His childhood was depressing and the list was long
From an uncle's juke box he learned Hank William's songs

He hated the rose fields, bending his back in the hot Texas sun
His father's leather belt struck fear whenever he encountered some fun

Ran away from home after birthday fifteen
Found life at a carnival though money was quite lean

Ernest learned to sell the public with his mind and his tongue
Grew up fast and never seemed young

Traveled the towns and back ways and alleys
Spent a stretch in the slammer in the San Fernando valley

When he was sprung he found work in a kitchen
Bourbon Street cafe where the women were witchy

Witnessed some voodoo during a hurricane season
High tailed it to the Rockies never said the reason

Worked three years on a ranch western slope winters
Hunted herds of elk listened to the wind when it whispers

Made it to Frisco and got real drunk for a time
Down in North Beach he lost every dime

Spent some time in Europe and developed a certain taste
Came back and made a pile of money could never be traced

He read multitudes of books kept and open mind
Everybody agreed to humans he was kind

Told hundreds of stories and many of them true
Hesby was his name and his legend always grew

Old Photographs and Wild Dreams

ERNEST HESBY

part three

In those golden days of Elvis
flat tops and good factory jobs

An old doctor hired Ernest to work
in Africa, Nigeria I believe

Disease, heat, bugs and wild animals
(that sort of thing)

Traveling circus of research teams
dissecting dead animals – sick, bloody stench

Ernest's main task was following them around
collecting guts, blood, some organs

Later the doctors studied them, analyzed them, wrote
papers about them – at night

At night Ernest would wash the blood and guts
off and dress up for the times

Go into a local village and drink the local brew
listen to hunters tell stories, eat some goat

He flirted would some African girls, said he
fell in love with one once

She was a farmer's daughter and the farmer
wanted him to stay and marry her

Ernest disappeared – back in the good old USA
lived to tell the story – barely

Old Photographs and Wild Dreams

ERNEST HESBY

part four

One dreary cold afternoon
Ernest and Newman drank cold beer and shared
hot wings

Ernest confided
his dreams or nightmares, big bad monstrous dreams
or nightmares

Biblical times
Old Testament and such, only not Israel or Palestine
or even Mesopotamia

Africa
he was among hundreds of slaves
white slaves

A sea of
white bodies, near nude, sweating and cutting
trees

With only
crude flint saws and vine like ropes, they toiled
exquisite misery

Thirsty, hungry
beyond belief he snapped- black nights ending
with bull whip mornings

diabolical hours
feces, pain doing back breaking labor
the end is near

The sky
so gray and hopeless...slowly got lighter and then
much lighter

Ernest
woke up and went to the bathroom, which is why he
told this tale

Right before
he arose from his stool and headed for the
men's room

part five

Spring arrived and Ernest
talked about his farm

Back in Illinois, he claimed, sat a
house full of Victorian charm

Corn and soybeans, with an oil
well or three

Won it in a card game in Chicago
don't you see

That explained his interest in crop prices
per bushel

Ernest seemed knowledgeable, even quite
official

He confided the government subsides checks
were large with figures quite nice

Oil money from OPEC paid for his fun at The
Tavern because of the current price

One day he planned a trip back there just to
see it all once again

He invited Newman to help drive him there and
meet all the farmer men

They talked in length about the times and when
they would soon depart

Broke down every detail and scoured the coming
weather charts

You may be wondering how that adventurous trip
turned out that year?

We'll get to all that later, let's order another
round of beer

ERNEST HESBY

part six

On a Tavern afternoon, when conversations lagged
and troubles weren't so much

The talk turned lively toward socialism, capitalism
and such

Ernest took the reins and bragged how Norway got
it right

Carl was from New Orleans and said they were commies,
hated their godless bite

Newman, he kept quiet, smelling fear from his ignorance,
decided to observe from afar

The heat turned up as Hesby grew loud and stood up to
address the entire bar

"Education and Doctors, and a culture that
treats humans like their brothers

Carl, red faced, screamed "they don't believe in
God!" who had heard this from his mother

Carl took another shot and declared all those
dead beats on welfare are just lazy

Ernest paid his tab, gave his middle finger, and as
he left muttered "he's just crazy"

Newman felt embarrassed, for no apparent reason,
but a kinship to Ernest

Carl said nothing as he washed glasses and wiped
the bar seeming kind of nervous

There's a host of subjects to avoid when folks drink and
get into a funky mood

Politics, religion, secrets, modern trends are just a few
that will fire up a bar time feud

Old Photographs and Wild Dreams

part seven

Deep in the beer
                Saturday afternoon
Newman wore a fresh haircut
                Ernest rubbed his scalp
Hesby, animated and frisky
                spoke of clouds and the past
Carnival life in his tender years
                freak shows and hucksters
Long train rides in the
                dark night
Tasting cheap whiskey
                day old hot dogs
Florida to Indiana
                westward to the Rockies
Ernest learned the value of a dollar
                true friends as well
Moving and traveling
                lit the wires of his soul
Out in California he stole a truck
                (not really)
Shared the blame with another carny
                from Colorado
Hard months in prison
                life was understood
Sometimes glorious and other times
                very unfair
The story caused Newman to cry
                later, at home

Old Photographs and Wild Dreams

part eight

Ernie held secrets

haunted...dark

Gaps in his life

love, romance, summer
in Greece

Lived alone...loved to hang with
bar flies

Or alone in his truck
driving

By the river banks

Knew many foods...and their delights

Persian...Indian

Thai and East Texan

Hamburgers-Rocky Road

Solid gold...to his friends

Respect...love...fear

Old Photographs and Wild Dreams

ERNEST HESBY

part nine

Books, books, books

Hesby and books

Newman met the books...borrowed them

Returned a few

Desolation Angels...sad prose

Dharma Bums...sleeping in box cars

Grapes of Wrath...depression blues

Good Earth...Pearl's best

Holmes on Baker Street

Nabokov's Pale Fire

Henry's Under Paris Rooftops

Vachss' Burke

Long hours at The Tavern

Endless discussions of plots

Air full of words

Trips to book stores

Lives changing

Old Photographs and Wild Dreams

part ten

Newman bore fresh news
                    hoped all would be glad
Bought the bar a round
                    the knowledge became unclad
Most were thrilled and a few just didn't care
                    Carl shook his hand, asked 'when and where?'
After the celebrations and the liquor was all bought
                    Everyone wondered, what Hesby thought?
His eyes and smile spoke goodness for his daily friend
                    But he knew change to his routine to attend
Newman left that night, goodbyes were said to all
                    Some of Hesby died as afternoons seemed to crawl
A year or three went by and Newman heard the news
                    Ernest Hesby died from sadness and the blues
Realization came heavy and memories triggered tears
                    Newman's life expanded from those Tavern years

Old Photographs and Wild Dreams

Since the days of slaves
in that region

A different style of humanity
grows there

A real Texas individual
poor and dishonest sometimes

Woods full of bootleggers
dry counties

Thousands of tiny churches
hellfire and brimstone

At the core of this peach:
G L Sellers

Tall, rail thin, bald and ageless
grinning, nodding

Part man of God, part con man
the seed of the peach

A sound heart containing goodness
also some miscellaneous parts

A tree trimmer and curb painter
"Old Feather Legs"

Nicknamed his way through life
"Hoehandle"

Lover of Gospel music
and dirty words

Husband to a red headed woman
"Sister Sellers"

He was "Brother" on Sundays
George on ocassion

Drove 30 mph on the Interstate
East Texas seed

Didn't love money
but had a few bucks

Considered dealing crack
tough economy

Love in his heart...East Texas
in his soul

child of the First War
                    God called to preach
old man by the seventies
                    short and stocky
trousers above the waist line
                    black suits
Colorado mountain pulpit
                    dour face
Preached Christ crucified
                    and risen
Shrill midwest voice
                    big visions
Wrote letters to the IRS
                    "Dear Dept KGB"
Bible in his mind
                    friendship in his heart
Plain and simple but comfortable
                    around the wealthy
Powerful in his meek ways
                    believed in fellowship
Like those who didn't agree
                    controversy
Uncanny and a mold breaker
                    walked the talk
Pastor Barnes to the multitudes
                    amen

Old Photographs and Wild Dreams

last eve I dreamt I spied old Bob

cruising down a Spanish cobblestone way

in a chariot wearing black robes

the wheels transformed into a rhythm of fire

the drainpipes so rusty sang his praises

charcoal gypsy maidens followed in his tracks

Spanish wind blew his wiry hair and his royal robes

his voice growled like rolling thunder

Bob pulled on the reins of the trojan horses

he stepped off and searched for an open pub

the crowded bar was stunned as he entered

he found a battered piano and took a seat

the music stopped the bar and they began a dance

profound words tumbled from his mouth

minds were altered as two siamese cats looked on

Old Photographs and Wild Dreams

SHOCK
SORROW
DISGUST
NAUSIA

crawling back through the damp weeds
and tangled undergrowth

this was his first but will never be his last

the scene will play over in his mind
like a broken projector

the face, the flash, it was over so quick

edged over to the dead man

HORROR
HOMESICK
REVULSION
GOD?

    Thoughts of thousands who sit in jails
or walk the executioner's path
for the same act

silly comedic – a medal will be pinned to his chest
for this unspeakable killing

eye for an eye?
        Then swift harsh punishment is soon
coming his way-

but it doesn't

Old Photographs and Wild Dreams

Pigeon Harold: They must have stayed late.

Pigeon Camille : Oh, the trade in, I see it.

Pigeon Harold : Pontiac Aztec...yuck!

Pigeon Camille : I kind of like it.

PH: I once heard that Pontiac had to apologize to Native Americans for naming it Aztec.

PC: Really?

PH: The US Military rejected it for aesthetic reasons alone.

PC: What day is it?

PH: Sunday, I think.

PC: Oh, that's why no one is here.

PH: I think they are going to fire Eddie.

PC: Oh, no, I like him. He's the only one who brings us corn.

PH: Yeah, but he's a lousy salesmen. Only got three cars out this month.

PC: Well, what do you want to do?

PH: Wait until tomorrow, see what happens.

PC: I'm hungry.

PH: Let's go over to Elm Street, see if Mrs. Gandy is up.

Old Photographs and Wild Dreams

The elder gunslinger rode the rocky trail
          at dawn the wet storm
               ceased
along with diamond hail

At the forest edge, a fork was revealed
          a crossroads it seemed
Once the old cowboy pulled the reins and stopped
          feeling unredeemed
He remembered the higher trail
          where safety, supplies, and fortune
lay ahead

Whereas, the lower fork led to a cold jail house
          bunk bed
          the hounds were close behind
          with hired hunters riding hard
A decision had to be birthed
          the result of an extra playing card
But the gunman was getting older
          his bones might not prevail
          lose his footing
          meet his maker
Minutes were ticking by
          the horse stomped and pawed the earth
A youthful urge grew inside him
          prison days were recalled
          the high trail just stood there
          began to speak

"C'mon you old hunter and mount up those snowy peaks"

Away they flew and down the trail they went
          the outcome is unknown
But the lifetime gambler understood
          life is but a loan

Old Photographs and Wild Dreams

Packards and faded LaSalles
rest on a muddy junkyard back acres
Kaisers mix rust with several Studebakers
missing their headlights

Oldsmobiles stare indignant at rusty Plymouths
who just smile
Pontiacs and DeSotos rub fenders with cordial attitudes
Mercurys lie peacefully beside a few Tuckers
while AMC's lust after DeLorean missing parts

A single wrecked Edsel mouths horror at the scene

God sheds a tear as the grass grows taller

Old Photographs and Wild Dreams

Diamond backed rattlers

hot sandstone valley

Indian fireworks stand

beer under the cooler

Beat up truck after truck

road full of dust

Ancient ceremony to full fill

a forgotten promise

High rocks hide the secret place

sundown signals the dozen

Or so warrior men

donning battle gear

Manning big leather drums

the smells of the fire crack

Create a nest of coals

cedar branches lay heavy

On the burning center

smoke flies upward

Choke, waft and climb

the line forms as the

Throaty call goes forth

until dawn they dance

Chant the life songs

new days ahead

But the past stays and lingers

Old Photographs and Wild Dreams

like it was yesterday...the pain...the hurt

oh how young and strong I was....no longer...never again

total loss of all I loved- no freedom- skinned alive

long cold days with desperate strangers...breakfast a 3 am...hog hair in the food

the horror of it all still boggles my mind...years later...water down the river

most scars have healed and been chalked up...still remember

Old Photographs and Wild Dreams

Year after year he smiles and sells
                    orange vest and winter shorts

Greenblatt kid from Brooklyn...Melrose Avenue
                    sandwich board life

Talent out the ass from piano to singing – comic
                    politico

Howard Stern's WACKPACK spitfire mouth piece...pot stirrer
                    Bobo & Mary Ann

No stranger to conflict...village town crier...MBA Cornell
                    Celebrity accountant

In spite of all the bluster, the sand paper beliefs- heart of pure gold
                    gifted entertainer

Larry inspires me when I see that smile- that GRIN

yes...he's notorious and I for one am glad he is...Keep
                    On
                    Being
                    Larry

Old Photographs and Wild Dreams

WILLIAM

Born McCarty, orphaned in the
Wild New Mexico Territory
Rode the outlaw trails

His legend grew into
a growing evolving story
Robbed a Chinese laundry

Hunger pains to a short
Sixteen-year-old boy
Killed a blacksmith in Arizona

But folks thought he
Wasn't so mean
William Bonney rode with cattle rustlers

Joined the Regulators
Killing spree
Many crimes

From Las Vegas
to New York
Papermen wrote

Bloody tales
Kid believed
He was a ghost

Never to be caught
Or jailed
Pat Garrett shot him

New Mexico grave
Buried him deep
Greasewood marker

Life was so short
A midnight flash
Infinite legend

Old Photographs and Wild Dreams

Matthew 5:45
ye may be the children of
your father (who is in heaven)
for he maketh the sun to rise
on the evil and the good
and sendeth rain upon the just
and the unjust...

...pouring rain – no quarters
tiny parking space- only be
a minute-

...gone for an hour...

NO TICKET

(rain would have washed it away anyway)

thoughts .....got away with something

GOOD

good for me ...the just?
(or am I unjust?)

Parking Police (without firearms) scowl
...unjust...they point at me...

(tables turned)

TICKET ON WET WINDSHIELD
with correct VIN and License plate

"...unjust I cry!...and (some indecent words too)

...who is just?

...who is unjust?

Old Photographs and Wild Dreams

All he had to do was get in his car
light a cigar...and drive to Jersey

A hero or a villain???
or a comedic chameleon?

A family man who...
walked never ran-

Made the Feds look
...like the bad guys

Tony held the power
killed by the hour

Carmela and the women
a crime boss's dilemma

He told the secrets
to Melfi (only)

Paulie Walnuts and Silvio
buried the ones we know

But Artie always fed
them as friends

Christopher and Adrianna
Mafia Americana

Both were severely dealt with
by Soprano

Tony and his paper
Zellman enabled the capers

Model neighbors
tomato growing Cusamanos

An American story
David Chase in his glory

Junior gave us sorrow
and hope for more tomorrow

Mob life at Bada Bing
goodbye we sing

Old Photographs and Wild Dreams

ripping and running....needle streets
Baltimore
Clint Eastwood duster...shotgun shine
underneath

"Omar coming!"

refusing profanity and a working class
life
tender hearted to his lovers and Christian
grandma
scarfaced to drug dealers- Barksdale and Stanfield crews
alike

"Omar coming!"

catlike moves and dark alley
beds
Prop Joe gave him the pager number
MURDER
student of mythology who shot and then
friended Brother Mouzone
together they joined forces and faced down
Stringer Bell

"Omar coming!"

torture of Butchie brought him back
Puerto Rico life
a simple child, Omar just glanced
the end of this mythical outlaw

"Omar coming!"

Old Photographs and Wild Dreams

Soft notes escaping from a Harlem window as big old
Buicks cruise down Fifth Avenue and go to dine at dance clubs
until dawn
Ella and the Count are everywhere and anywhere for hip cats
to dig and jump on
Golden horns mix the smoky air and squeeze the modern soul
as they yearn for the truth momma told them
Listen closely for a Blue Moon to saddle up the past with
real dollars and tiny income
Red rose gardens and whitewashed school books make no sense
in the cool refer nights
Forgetting the style and not caring for rules, the cats bob and weave
as the bats appear and give you a sweet bite
Jazz from the earth and jazz from the sky, calling for east and
calling for west
Drums beating loud for the cattle call that rounds up Harlem's
hep cat best
Soft notes escaping from an empty loft near the park then fall
on the sidewalk until the ghosts move along
Victrola heaven cranks orders from a magician's vocal chords
that tap out a broken heart's song
Get up right now and head for the store, the radio, or the smoky
old club
Your jazz is waiting patiently and you'll never have to show the man
your ticket stub

Old Photographs and Wild Dreams

from the ripe age of 12 he learned the craft and taught us miracles
that came under the headlines of JAZZ – gypsy jazz
the thunder that rang inside his sweet head later fetched
Stephane and his swinging violin to the stage
despite the caravan fire and the awful burns that lost
some fingers and feelings-
the guitar came first
music from European small cafes made the women dance and
whirl their skirts
Paris night clubs melted from the hot lights and sweaty crowds-
twirling his mustache and bending the strings all the while he was
smiling that smile
he knew something was happening
he changed us, the world and the way we think
from London stages and the lucky souls who saw and heard
his fast magic
Eddie Cantor kissed his hand and allowed the jazz to seep into
his pores and bones
played with the Duke at Carnegie Hall- bowed to cheering thousands
of New Yorkers
he played...God did he play...
a beatnik at heart he sometimes skipped concerts "to walk the beach" or
"smell the dew"
Sir, we owe you and a debt for your gifts and thank God
you made records

Old Photographs and Wild Dreams

Behind him in the shadowy corner
                    dim lit stage and a guitar
                               coax a steady melodic tone
...drink up ...have another one

she's gone- your fault...all your fault

people shuffle in and out ...some whistle and clap

the music

the jazz guitar

depressed and lonely he stays and drinks

                a friend drops by – who owes him a

                               sawbuck

he asks for another- and a drink

      his mind starts to drift inward toward the songs

whispers of dream clouds and beach days...sea shells

      a good woman and good whiskey

                    ....money to burn

the dark corner stops playing- silence is deafening

                still he stays and drinks

soon the break is over and the jazz heats up again

        until dawn...he leaves

                until tomorrow

Old Photographs and Wild Dreams

Roman soldier of Marcellus

expert on European fast food

Movies with a glass of beer

Opinions of female relationships

"he should have known"

Dark killer who winds and twists

down alleys of danger

lover of dope- at home and abroad

Pepsi challenge

Afraid of little and avid book reader-toilet

Amateur philosopher – curious about other's opinions
"Marvin, what do you think?"

Committed to "the life" even when it means his life

agnostic about miracles

very pro-pork...bacon's good

A real gentleman when it comes to the boss's wife

Jack Rabbit Slim's

Partner to Jules Winfield and dancer for the ages

"Butch"

Old Photographs and Wild Dreams

Anne Marie Burr
Lonnie Trumbell
Joni Lenz
Lynda Ann Healy
Donna Gail Manson
Susan Elaine Rancourt
Roberta Kathleen Parks
Brenda Carol Bull
Georgeann Hawkins
Janice Ott
Denise Naslund
Caryn Campbell
Julie Cunningham
Denise Lynn Oliverson
Melanie Cooley
Nancy Wilcox
Melissa Smith
Laura Aime
Debby Kent
Carol Da Ronch
Nancy Baird
Sure Curtis
Debbie Smith
Rita Lorraine Jolly
Vicki Lynn Hollar
Karen Chandler
Kathy Kleiner
Lisa Levy
Margaret Bowman
Cheryl Thomas
Kimberly Leach
Lynette Calver
Rita Carran

…..and probably many more

Old Photographs and Wild Dreams

Less Inebriated : You know, I've been thinking.

More Inebriated : Oh yeah? Good. I've been thinking too.

LI: Old Charley Manson really screwed things up for the hippies after all that blood thirst.

MI: What? You're kidding you moron. They were already messed up. Nobody like those lazy, dirty longhairs back then, and they ...they

LI: Shut up. Everybody loved those free love girls and the guys had some pretty great acid. Try to find anything free now, or acid.

MI: Okay, okay, maybe you've got a point there, but Charley Manson, really?

LI: Hell yes, Manson and whole damn family. Everybody in LA was scarred
shitless about those hippie freaks after all that.

MI: I don't know. He had a lot of other shit on his plate, like a life sentence, you know.

LI: You're missing my point, you idiot.

MI: So what?

Old Photographs and Wild Dreams

Early December, a Colorado snow on a Denver Post Tuesday

Oh, that was the day the music died for me

I won't talk about him, but time stood still- evil dawned hard

ROCKETS EXPLODED

wheels caught fire

mythical Gods retreated to
Babylon

why?why?why?why? The New York streets demanded......

Imagine was a prayer as worshippers banded together in the Park

Sadness devils camped around my heart and sand low

Black crepe hung heavy on the Dakota windows

Giant black crows stood watch high in the trees and murmured

"He's dead"

I heard the news today oh boy, and my soul disagreed

His records still held his voice and loud speakers shook the earth

Never understood or ever come to terms (or any rational terms)

what a country!

Old Photographs and Wild Dreams

School days...blurry daze,
many sad...mediocre moments

Retreat into books...paper route
highs and lows...Denison

End of segregation...change blowing
in Texas

New school...scary crowds...bigger in everyway
excitement?

Climbing stairs...exploring downtown streets
Watson's Drive-In

Eight grade history...lightning bolt to the brain
Mrs. Cooke

Attractive...powerful intelligence...interested in myself?
myself?

Worldly tongue with a unique cursive style-
became my own

Days became lighter ...books piled high
curiosity was birthed

The way she made her "E's"...her tolerant look
the elegant way she moved

Forged in my heart...lives in my soul...that particular
64

Old Photographs and Wild Dreams

out of Lebanon, Pa...to the rugged mines
of Leadville, Colorado- she held a large family
together- working hard was the norm- a
spiritual tornado

kind at heart and love in those blue eyes- saw
truth as she spent time in the kitchen- even
more in a mountain church prayer booth-
knew God well

happy without riches- never knew life that
was easy- family was her world- raised a
brood with the Bible- and respect for
others- meant what she said – had a listening
ear

recited poems at Christmas- welcome mat out
for strangers all year- Mary, we miss you and
your one of a kind familiar voice- Christmas
Eve never the same without your poems

Old Photographs and Wild Dreams

Oh! lovely Carolyn...mother to the Beats

lover to Kerouac

husband to Neal

University of Denver....met the mad Neal &
everything happened afterward

blonde beauty full of human jazz sheltering
the best qualities (and worst) of those poets
raising offspring of these unicorns

heart breaking years...zenith of her generation
fountain of love...Oh! Lovely Carolyn...
essential to Cassady & Kerouac

hundreds of miles and meals
referee to a fault...selfless lifetime
muse...portrait of wonder years
moving too fast

Oh! lovely Carolyn...centerpiece to "On
The Road" - San Francisco dame...
London bound as the rest of us tried
to dissect their relationships-
utter failure

Old Photographs and Wild Dreams

angel to a generation
                    -laid the anthem bricks
woodstock nation

canadian smile with a wooden guitar
                              -blonde waif
voice like a dulcimer

...many did not listen to her soft heartbeat

.......her big yellow taxi : transported the Ladies
                              of the Canyon

pastel painting of North Country

                    words

tamed the tiger...collaborated with Mingus
                                   the
                                      genius

God's a bogie man...folk songs or jazz- indefinable

                    court n spark

nothing like her before or after...
                         confused
                              disillusionment

.....when the dust finally settled...she
                              reigns
on Both Sides Now

Old Photographs and Wild Dreams

rice is nice but in a pudding
                    superb
puddings are fine but with rice, a healing
                              herb
dreamland puddings con rice transforms into a flotation
                    device
smooth and creamy the dish is supreme with
                    rice
hot or cold, the familiar flavor unfolds and
                              satisfies
rice is nice but in a pudding superbly
                    rice....

Old Photographs and Wild Dreams

Oh! but if I could sculpt a statue

one of silver or of gold

One that would endure the ages

never would grow old

I'd carve one of a sideshow barker

in front of his massive tents

I'd carve his deep expressions : his showmanship

with all its carnival intents

For the Sideshow holds a place in my life

deep within my heart

This eclectic nome for a publisher: who has done

what others never even start

My books all bear its brand, it soul,

feel and touch

Without the Sideshow, my enduring journey

wouldn't amount to very much

Old Photographs and Wild Dreams

In Persian the meaning is ... child
of light

How fitting...how appropriate

        sweet mother-in-law

    forgiveness

      love

        mercy

          courage

      loyal

Not enough ...words

     servant of God...disciple of light

Sincere blood pulses inside her- Rita- avid listener

        compassionate understanding

           brilliant smile

Child of light ...yet still so very human

         Matriarch to a family...God's
                Gift

My life would be less, much less...if I never knew

       Her

Old Photographs and Wild Dreams

WRONGFULLY CONVICTED

please read his tragic, yet true story :

jacknissalkeisinnocent.wordpress.com

Old Photographs and Wild Dreams

WRONGFULLY CONVICTED

please read this tragic, yet true story at :

kennethandersenisinnocent.com

Old Photographs and Wild Dreams

Poetry has always worn a broad definition, depending
on the poet, the reader, or the critic. My own is that
singular kernel of thought, or ordinary beauty that
inspires if only for a moment. My style evolved from
a life of self-search to understand who I was or who I
felt under this mask of humanity. Who am I? Viewpoints
are skewed by this quest.

I was born John Kenneth Prindle. When I was two,
my parents divorced and my father went home to
Minnesota. My mother stayed in Texas and when I
was five, she met and married Leo Bucher. He adopted
me. He was a kind and loving father and I miss him
terribly. However, I often wondered about my biological
father, whose genes, DNA, and blood line was pumping
inside me. When I got married and had children, it
bothered me more than I expected that he chose to remain
out of my life.

Years later, some questions were answered. I reconnected
with my cousins in Minnesota and visited them. They filled
in a lot of unknown about him and in return, myself to a degree.
This past year, my oldest son gifted me with a DNA test and
more answered came in the light of day. The broad results were
I am 99.5 % European. The breakdown was 74.7 % British& Irish,
12.7% French & German. At first, that was all I had. I pursued the
Irish link with exuberance and relished the Irish poetry and its
rich history. I was happy.

I later pursued the Prindle genealogy through Ancestry and more clues
were unearthed. I am a direct descendant of William Prindle, the
first Prindle to arrive in 1643. He settled in a Newtown, Connecticut, and
raised a family that spread out over the colony. The Prindles ended up
moving to Sandgate, Vermont and were among the founding families
there. One of my great grandfathers was Zalmon Prindle, a soldier in the
Revolutionary War. Several of our cousins died in the war giving birth
to our nation. The Prindles would eventually move to Minnesota, where
my father was born. Once again, I was happy.

But wait, there's more. Ancestry linked me to where William was from and that turned out of be Midlothian, Scotland. Our original name in 1200's
was Hoppringle and we settled in the Scottish Borderlands. Hoppringle was
the name of a ridge separating the rivers Armet and Todhole. The name evolved into Pringle and Prindle but were all the same clan. Prindles and Pringles still live in Scotland and have their own castles, crests, and customs.
One of my great grandfathers was Sir James Prindle, a Scottish knight. I am still learning more about my family and who I am. In closing, I lift a toast to the Prindles of Scotland.

"May the best you've ever seen
be the worst you'll ever see;
May a moose ne'er leave yer girnal
Wi' a teardrop in his e'e.
May ye aye keep hale and hearty
Till ye're auld enough tae dee,
May ye aye be just as happy
As I wish ye aye tae be."